SPACE BLOG

Angela Royston

Author: Angela Royston
Editor: Kathy Middleton
Production coordinator: Ken Wright
Prepress technician: Margaret Amy Salter
Series consultant: Gill Matthews

Picture Credits:
ESA: 13, 23, Hinode JAXA/NASA/PPARC 11
NASA: (Cover) 4b, 5, 8, 14, 19, 21, 26b, The Hubble Heritage Team, STScI, AURA, Amy Simon Cornell 16, JPL 9, 15, 17, 18, 22, 24, JPL/Cornell University/Maas Digital 27, JPL/USGS 26t, Kennedy Space Center 6b, Visible Earth 4t, 31 Royal Swedish Academy of Sciences 10b
Shutterstock: (Cover) Catmando 25, Norma Cornes 29, Chris Harvey 7, Sebastian Kaulitzki 10t, Byron W. Moore 12, Rafael Pacheco 6t, Sabino Parente 20, Elisei Shafer 28, Sashatverdy 5t.
Illustrations: Geoff Ward

Library and Archives Canada Cataloguing in Publication

Royston, Angela
Space blog / Angela Royston.

(Crabtree connections)
Includes index.
ISBN 978-0-7787-9910-8 (bound).--ISBN 978-0-7787-9931-3 (pbk.)

1. Space flights--Anecdotes--Juvenile literature. 2. Manned space flight--Anecdotes--Juvenile literature. 3. Outer space--Exploration--Anecdotes--Juvenile literature. I. Title. II. Series: Crabtree connections

TL793.R69 2010 j629.45 C2010-905075-4

Library of Congress Cataloging-in-Publication Data

Royston, Angela, 1945-
Space blog / Angela Royston.
p. cm. -- (Crabtree connections)
Includes index.
ISBN 978-0-7787-9931-3 (pbk. : alk. paper) -- ISBN 978-0-7787-9910-8 (reinforced library binding : alk. paper)
1. Space flights--Anecdotes--Juvenile literature. 2. Manned space flight--Anecdotes--Juvenile literature. 3. Outer space--Exploration--Anecdotes--Juvenile literature. I. Title.
TL793.R6187 2011
629.45--dc22

2010030825

Crabtree Publishing Company
www.crabtreebooks.com 1-800-387-7650

Printed in the U.S.A./082010/WO20101210

Published in Canada
Crabtree Publishing
616 Welland Ave.
St. Catharines, Ontario
L2M 5V6

Published in the United States
Crabtree Publishing
PMB 59051
350 Fifth Avenue, 59th Floor
New York, New York 10118

Toni Omari's Space Mission

My crew and I have just lifted off from Cape Canaveral to start the most unbelievable journey. I am setting off in an incredible spacecraft on a tour of our **solar system**. I'll **orbit** the Sun and land on the most interesting **planets** and **moons**. This blog will report the highlights and the hazards.

Earth, as seen from space

10, 9, 8...

Liftoff went according to plan. First there was the countdown. When the count hit 4, the engines roared, the spacecraft shuddered and, as the count reached zero, it slowly lifted off the ground.

This rocket is as big as a skyscraper. It is filled mostly with fuel.

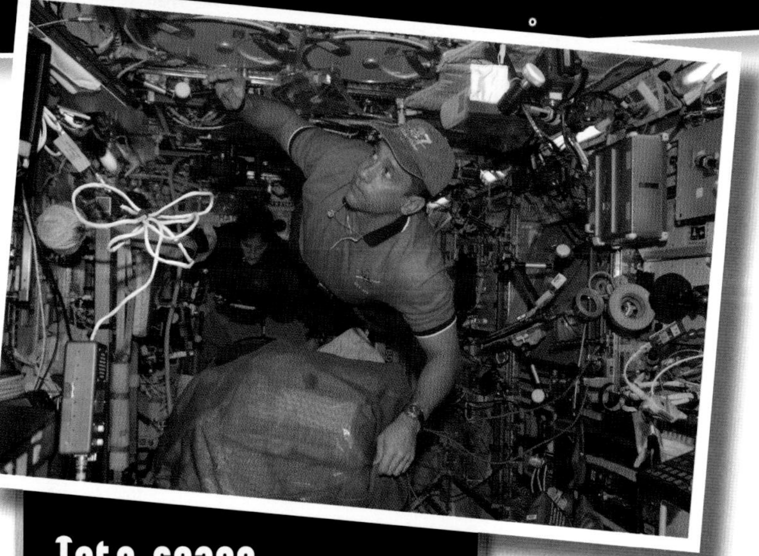

This astronaut is carrying out repairs as he floats inside his spacecraft.

Into space

After just a few minutes, the spacecraft had left the **atmosphere**, and we were in space. I looked through the window and watched Earth getting smaller. I undid my seatbelt and, without the pull of Earth's **gravity**, I immediately began to float. I pushed myself around the spacecraft—our home for the next several years.

DATA UPDATE

To leave Earth, a spacecraft has to escape the force of gravity, the pull that exists between any two objects. Large objects, such as Earth, exert a stronger pull than small objects. The Sun is so immense, the pull of its gravity keeps the planets in orbit around it.

This is a map of the solar system.

First Stop—the Moon

Yesterday we landed on the Moon, Earth's nearest neighbor. As we flew low over rocks and **craters**, a **meteorite** hit the ground. It crashed right in front of us, making another crater! We landed where the first astronauts landed years ago, in 1969.

The Moon's surface is totally bare, except for the many craters made by meteorites crashing into it.

The first astronauts to walk on the Moon planted an American flag there.

Stepping out

I put on my spacesuit, checked that the air supply was working, and stepped outside. There is no air on the Moon. Without my spacesuit, I would have died instantly. First, I photographed the flag and the footprints made in the dust by the first astronauts on the Moon. The footprints looked as if they had been made only yesterday.

Gravity rocks

Then I had some fun with gravity, which is only one-sixth as strong as on Earth. I hurled a rock as far as I could, and it arced high into the sky before it slowly fell to the ground. It landed 990 feet (300 meters) away. Then I jumped 20 feet (six meters) off the ground! After about an hour, I hopped back to my spacecraft and took off.

DATA UPDATE

The Moon has no atmosphere, so there is no wind or rain to disturb the dust. Without air there is no sound—meteorites crash in silence.

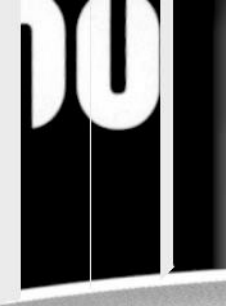

This morning we reached Venus, the nearest planet to Earth, although it couldn't really be more different. Its poisonous atmosphere, which is 100 times thicker than Earth's, traps the Sun's heat but blocks out its light.

Dangerous descent

We descended through the bright yellow clouds of **sulphuric acid** and landed. The weight of the atmosphere pressing on the spacecraft made it creak alarmingly. I put on a **reinforced** spacesuit, which is as heavy as a suit of armor, and clambered outside.

SPACE WARNING

Venus's atmosphere is mainly carbon dioxide, the gas that is causing **global warming** on Earth. Unless global warming is halted, Earth could eventually become poisoned and barren like Venus.

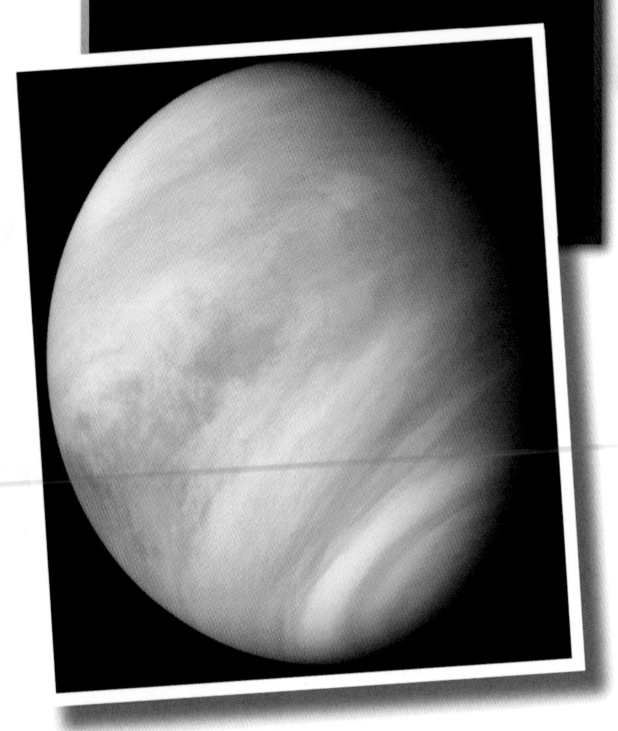

Venus is surrounded by thick yellow clouds.

Maat Mons is one of Venus's many volcanoes.

SPACE TIP

Don't ever spend a whole day on Venus. The atmosphere is so thick it makes the planet spin more slowly. A day here lasts 243 Earth days, the longest in the solar system.

Volcanoes galore

I was sweating. Was it because Venus is the hottest planet in the solar system? Or was it fear? If my spacesuit crumpled, I would be dead in seconds. Through the dim light, I spotted the battered remains of a spacecraft. That was enough for me! I hauled myself back into the spacecraft, and, as we took off, I glimpsed one of Venus's spectacular volcanoes. It made my visit worthwhile!

The Mighty Sun

From Venus, we headed straight to the Sun, the center of our solar system. The Sun is a million times bigger than Earth and its surface is a thousand times hotter. It is so hot, we couldn't go closer than 620,000 miles (1,000,000 kilometers).

The Sun is a giant ball of burning gas.

SPACE WARNING

Looking at the Sun, even all the way from Earth, can damage your eyes. Now, imagine being close up to the Sun. You need super strong goggles to protect your eyesight!

Sunspots

Even from this distance, the Sun was spectacular. The surface was covered with dark sunspots and flames licked 6,200 miles (10,000 kilometers) into the outer atmosphere.

Sunspots are dark because they are slightly cooler than their surroundings.

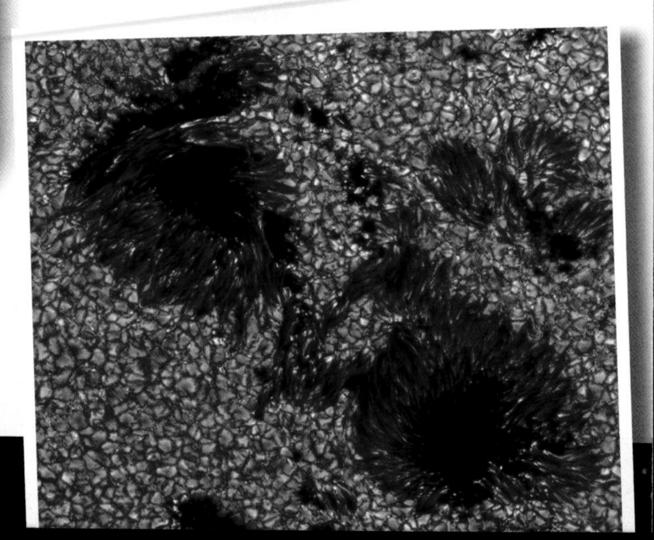

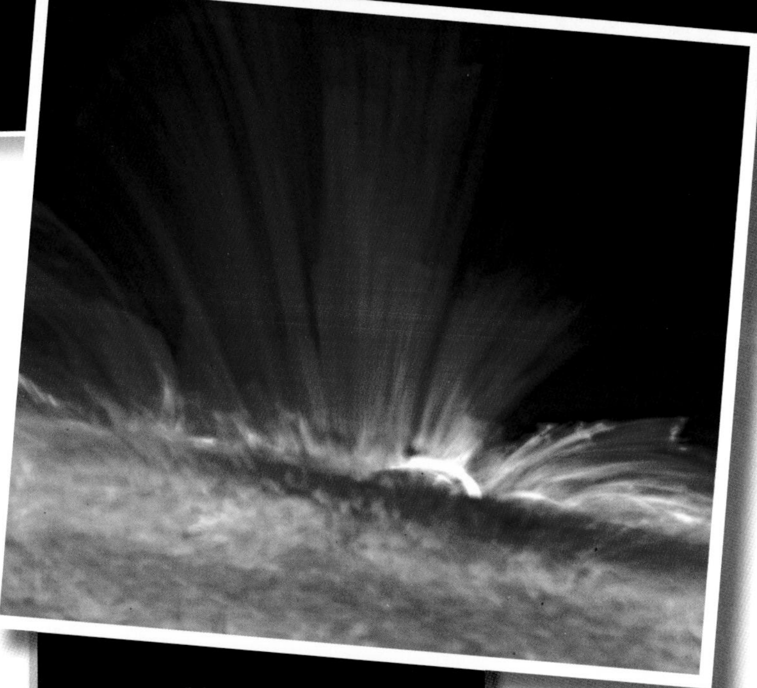

A solar flare erupts from the upper layer of the Sun's atmosphere.

Solar flares

Solar flares are vast **eruptions** of hot gases that explode into space. They produce streams of **solar particles** that travel beyond Earth. Suddenly a warning sounded in the spacecraft. A shower of solar particles was heading our way! Those lethal, high-energy particles just missed us.

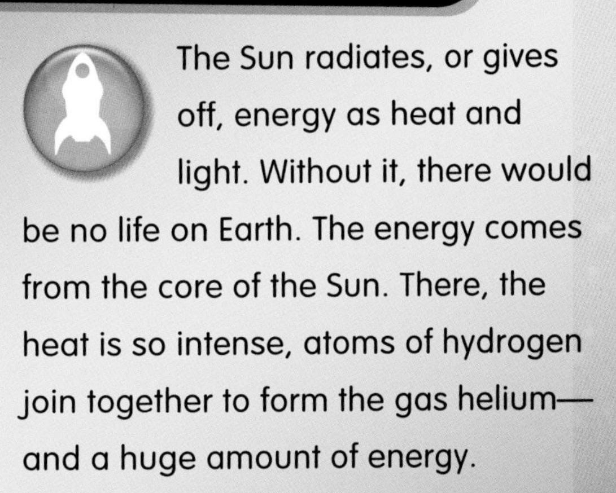

DATA UPDATE

The Sun radiates, or gives off, energy as heat and light. Without it, there would be no life on Earth. The energy comes from the core of the Sun. There, the heat is so intense, atoms of hydrogen join together to form the gas helium—and a huge amount of energy.

Mercury

We orbited right around the Sun and then set off towards Mercury. Instead of landing on this tiny planet, we swooped down low and had a good look at it through my binoculars.

Melting metal

Mercury is closest to the Sun so during the day it is fiercely hot. However, it is not as hot as Venus. I spotted the remains of Mariner, the first **unmanned** spacecraft to land on Mercury. There wasn't much left of this **space probe** because it had almost melted in the blistering heat.

Mercury is much smaller than Earth and has no atmosphere, water, or life.

DATA UPDATE

A **comet** is a huge snowball of frozen water and dust. Most comets orbit the Sun in long, oval orbits.

Halley's comet takes 76 years to orbit the Sun. Some comets take hundreds of years.

Close call with a comet

As we sped on towards Jupiter, we were almost hit by a comet! I noticed a white cloud rushing up behind us and quickly steered to one side. I just made it in time to watch the comet's frozen core of dust and ice slide past. It was followed by its great, steamy tail—6,200 miles (10,000 kilometers) long.

SPACE TIP

Orbiting a big object is like whirling something around your head before letting it go—it increases the speed. Orbiting the Sun has given me enough speed to reach Jupiter, 496 million miles (779 million kilometers) away.

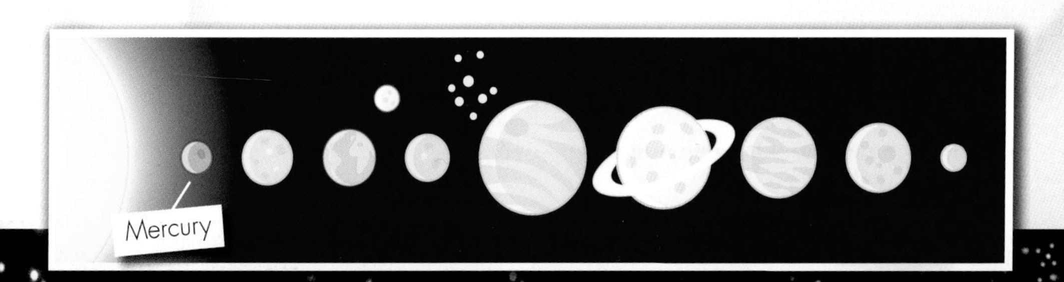

Dodging Asteroids

Yesterday we crossed the **asteroid** belt, a wide band of millions of asteroids that orbit the Sun between the inner and outer planets. We had to steer our way through them!

Alarming asteroids!

I kept my eyes peeled and swerved from side to side to avoid crashing into these lumps of rock. Then a large asteroid zapped into view! I bounced off its side, before dodging around another two smaller asteroids.

SPACE WARNING

Some asteroids wander through space. You could meet one almost anywhere. Sometimes an asteroid collides with a moon or planet and crashes into its surface. Many scientists think the dinosaurs became extinct because an asteroid crashed into Earth, creating a dust cloud that blocked out the Sun.

Asteroids are covered in craters, made when one asteroid crashes into another.

In February 2001, the space probe NEAR Shoemaker landed on an asteroid. NEAR stands for Near Earth Asteroid Rendezvous.

DATA UPDATE

Most asteroids are rocks usually just a few feet or miles long. At least 200 are over 62 miles (100 kilometers) long. Ceres, which measures 580 miles (933 kilometers) across, is the largest asteroid and is classed as a small planet.

Moving on...

Having left the four inner, rocky planets behind, our spacecraft is now heading toward the outer planets. We've been to Venus and seen Mercury, and plan to visit Mars on our way back to Earth.

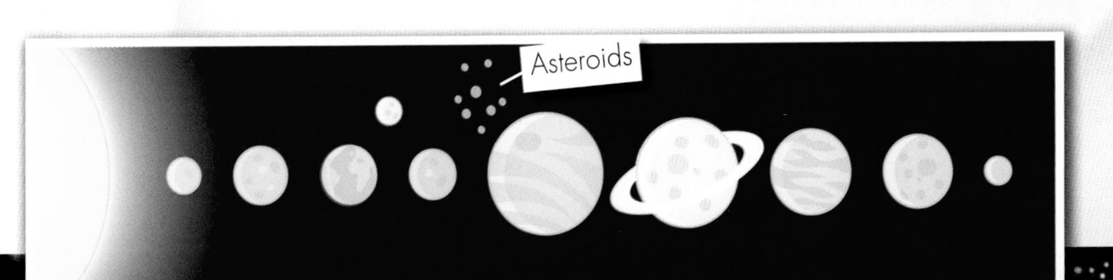

Jupiter

After a long journey, we have reached Jupiter, the biggest planet in the solar system. It measures 87,000 miles (143,000 kilometers) across and is bigger than all the other planets put together. All we can see are its striped bands of clouds.

The colored bands of clouds are caused by different chemicals in the atmosphere. The white outermost clouds are crystals of ammonia.

No place to land

We can't land here because this giant planet is nearly all hydrogen gas. Beneath the deep atmosphere, scientists think there is probably an ocean of liquid hydrogen. It's not a place to visit. Jupiter spins so fast its atmosphere is whipped into strong winds of 403 miles (650 kilometers) per hour. This makes a hurricane on Earth look like a breeze.

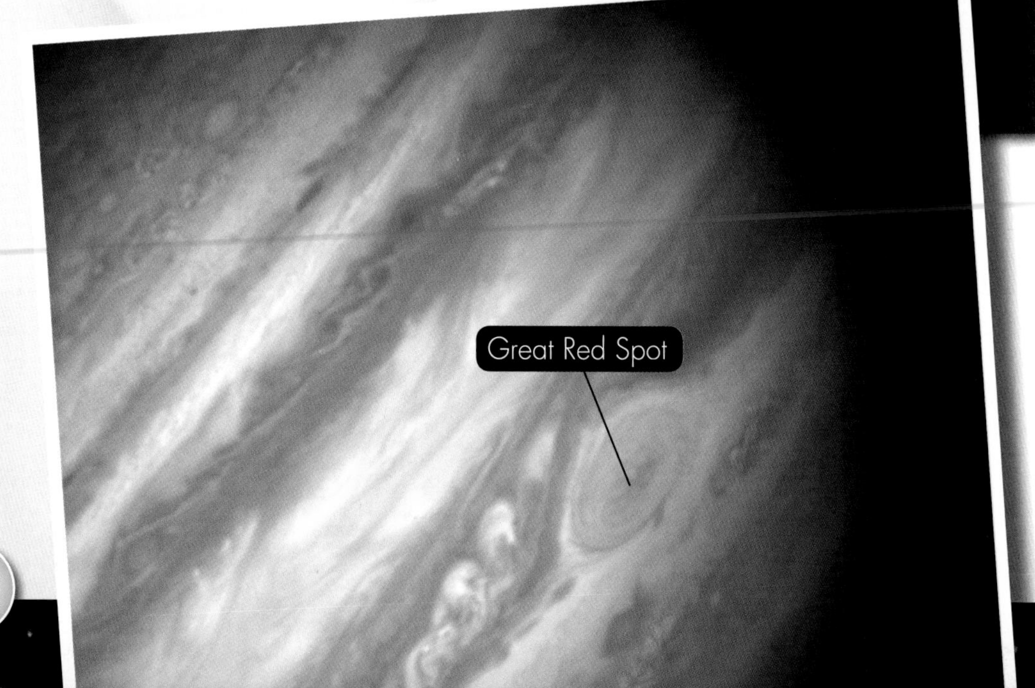

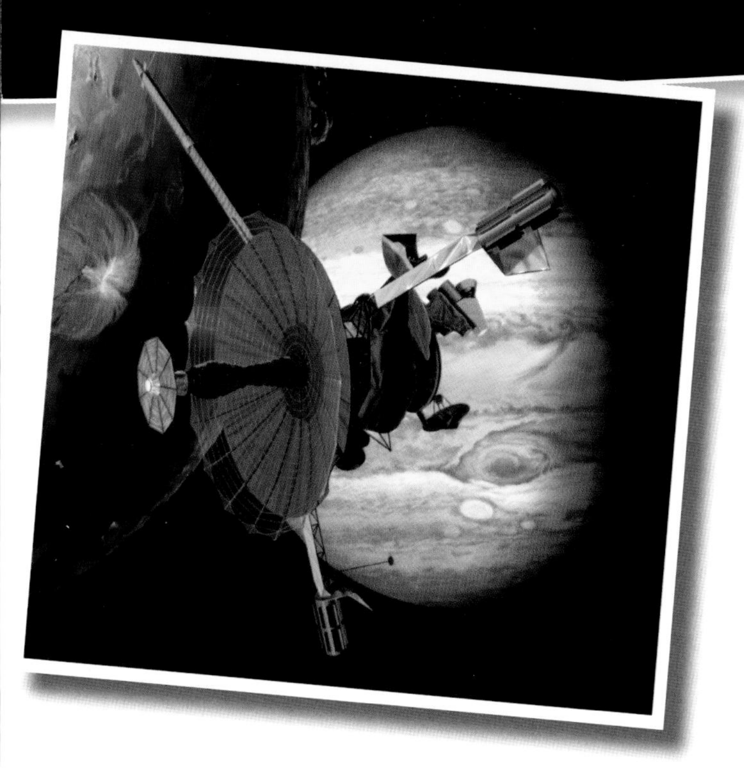

An illustration shows the Galileo space probe.

SPACE TIP

Don't get too close to the Great Red Spot. It is a mega storm that can suck you in. I flew through the towering tops of Jupiter's clouds and examined it from a safe distance.

DATA UPDATE

In the 1990s, the United States' unmanned space probe Galileo plunged into Jupiter's atmosphere and orbited the planet for several years. When it ran out of fuel in 2003, it fell through the atmosphere and burned up.

Jupiter has at least 63 moons, but we headed straight for the two that excited us the most, Io and Europa. Our first stop was on Io, Jupiter's nearest moon. It's the most colorful place in the solar system. I was desperate to get out of the spacecraft and onto firm ground again.

Volcanic gunk

Io is covered with active volcanoes. The one we landed on suddenly started spouting a plume of smelly yellow sulphur.

DATA UPDATE

Scientists think that there is a warm ocean beneath Europa's icy surface. The moon also has a thin atmosphere that contains oxygen. The big question is, could there be life beneath the surface?

Io is colorful but dangerous. It has more active volcanoes than anywhere else in the solar system.

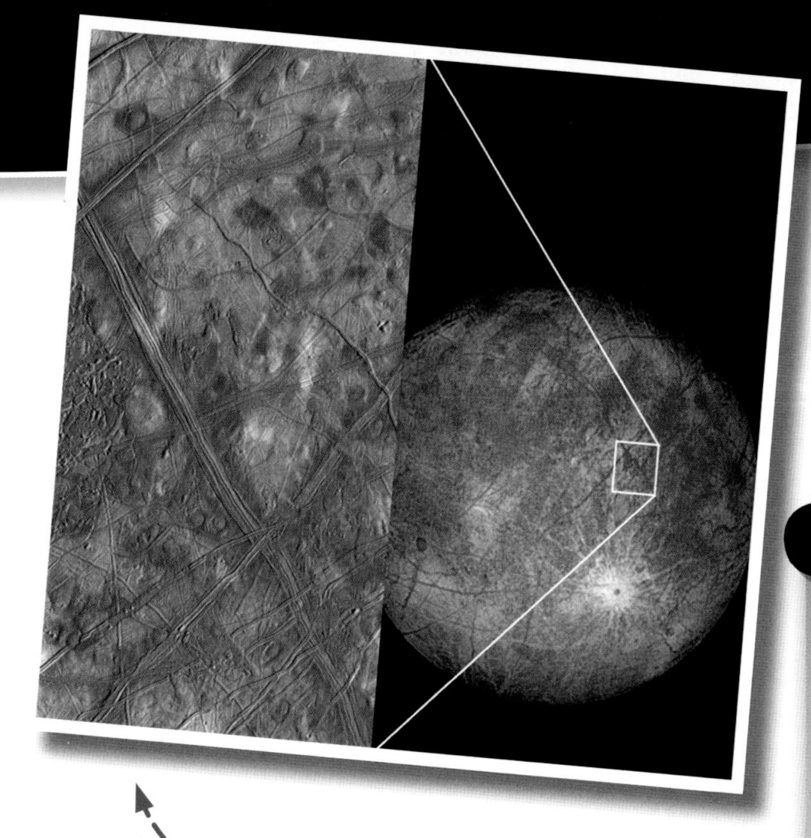

Galileo took these photos of Europa. The area in the white box is enlarged on the left.

Europa

Yesterday, we landed on Europa, the moon that scientists are most interested in. It is totally different from Io. The surface, which is very flat and very cold at –392°F (–200°C), looks very much like sea ice. We skidded to a halt and stepped carefully on to the ice.

SPACE TIP

Io is covered with different kinds of **lava**. They include:

- yellow-white crunchy powder
- black tar
- sticky brown gunk
- lakes of liquid sulphur

Don't get stuck in the brown gunk!

Distant Pluto

We've just arrived at the edge of the solar system. We are now 2,280 million miles (3,670 million kilometers) from the Sun. It is so far away that the Sun is just another star in the night sky.

Easy does it...

I landed on the rocky surface this morning, but I had to be careful. Pluto is smaller than Earth's Moon. It is so small, its gravity is very weak. I could hardly keep my feet on the ground and nearly floated into outer space!

The temperature on the surface of Pluto is a toe-curling -382°F (-230°C).

DATA UPDATE

Pluto is part of the Kuiper Belt, thousands of extremely cold rocks that orbit the most distant parts of the solar system. Pluto's classification as a planet was changed to a dwarf planet in 2006, when the **Hubble space telescope** spotted larger, more distant rocks in the Kuiper Belt.

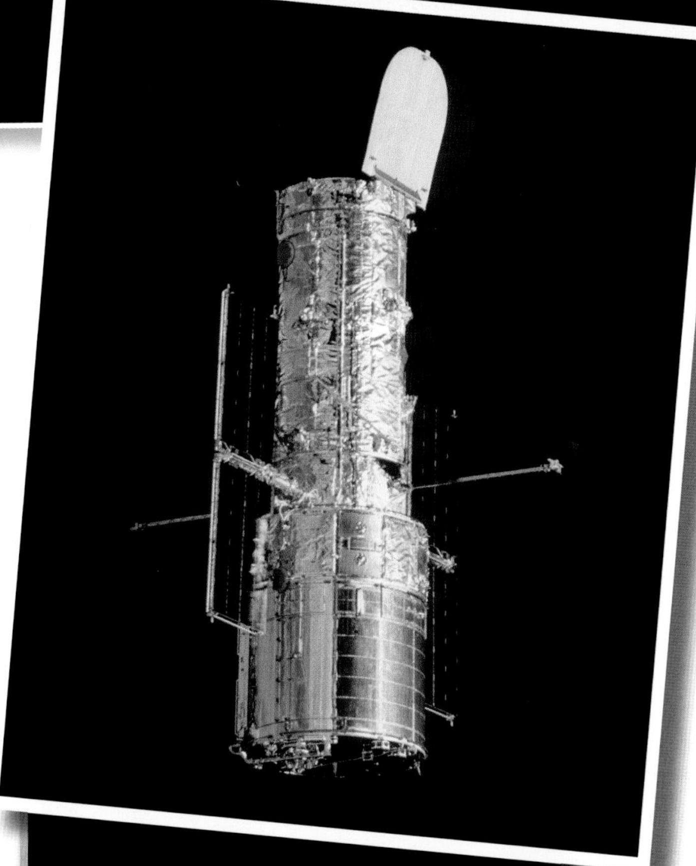

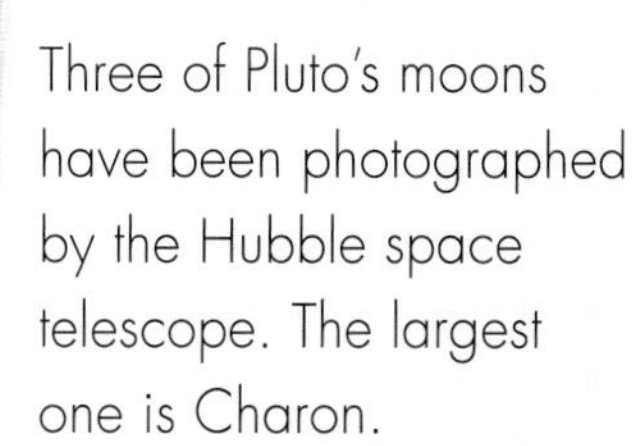

Three of Pluto's moons have been photographed by the Hubble space telescope. The largest one is Charon.

SPACE TIP

You can't spend too long on Pluto—it is freezing! Pluto is 40 times farther from the Sun than Earth, which makes it a very cold planet.

Moon gazing

I took a look at Charon, Pluto's moon. It is about half the size of Pluto and the largest object you can see from here. I didn't spend much time moon gazing—I couldn't wait to start the journey home.

Saturn

At last, after a very long and boring journey, we have arrived at Saturn. This pale giant is the second biggest planet and has a fantastic ring system.

DATA UPDATE

Saturn is 795 million miles (1,280 million kilometers) from Earth. The Cassini-Huygens space probe, launched from Earth in October 1997 took 6 years, 8 months, and 2 weeks to get here.

Rings of ice

The seven wide, flat rings are amazing to fly over, particularly the outer ring. This contains the largest chunks of ice. We followed one chunk, as it jostled its way around the planet. Then we skimmed across the tops of the other rings to the inner ring. This has mainly dust-sized specks of ice.

Saturn's rings are less than 1.86 miles (3 kilometers) deep and the largest chunks of ice measure about 10 feet (3 meters) across.

Saturn consists mainly of hydrogen, the lightest substance of all. This makes Saturn very light for its enormous size.

Storm clouds

After the rings, we dipped into the white outer clouds of ammonia crystals, but we didn't dive too deep. Like Jupiter, Saturn's atmosphere is whipped into hurricane winds. It is also ripped by violent lightning, particularly around the **equator**. Tomorrow we will set off for Titan, Saturn's largest moon.

SPACE TIP

Saturn's rings are definitely the best ones to explore. Neptune has rings as well as Saturn, but they are thinner and less spectacular. Even Jupiter has a thin ring, but it is very difficult to see.

Saturn's Best Moon

I dropped down through bright orange clouds to land on Titan, a moon of ice and methane. When I first saw this remarkable moon, I thought for a moment I had arrived back on Earth.

Familiar-looking landscape

The land is broken by hills, valleys, and plains and crossed by rivers that flow into lakes and seas. But the hills are made of ice, not rock, and the rivers and seas are filled with methane, not water. Titan is so cold that methane, which is a gas on Earth, is a liquid here. Of course, no trees, plants, or any animals can possibly live here.

SPACE WARNING

Titan's clouds consist of methane and ethane gas, both of which burn easily. The gases don't catch fire here, because the atmosphere has no oxygen. Your space pack has oxygen, so make sure none of it escapes!

Titan's "pebbles" consist of ice. The "soil" is methane dust.

The surface of Titan looks surprisingly similar to a rocky coast on Earth.

Bone-freezing

I put on my extra-warm spacesuit and stepped outside. I breathed in oxygen from my space pack and thought about home. When I cross Jupiter's orbit on the way back home, I will be almost halfway there.

DATA UPDATE

In 2004, the Cassini-Huygens unmanned space probe orbited Titan and mapped its surface. Then the space probe Huygens detached and landed, sending amazing photos back to Earth.

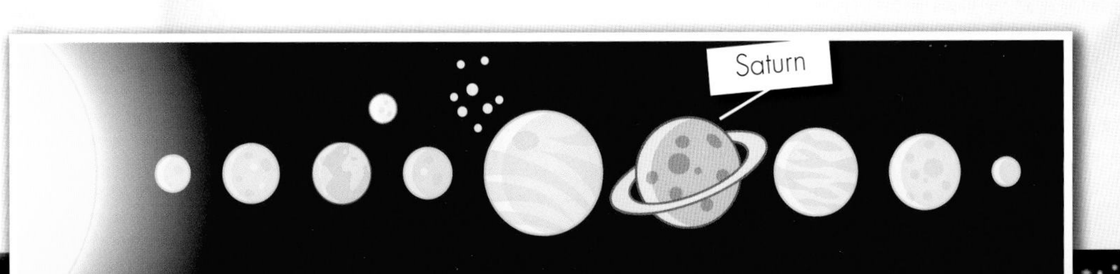

Mars

Yesterday we reached Mars, the last stop on our epic journey. This rocky planet is "next door" to Earth, but we still have a long way to go before reaching home. The landscape is spectacular! We flew past Olympus Mons, the highest volcano in the solar system, and landed close to the longest canyon, Valles Marineris.

Great canyon

I put on my spacesuit and stepped out, eager to explore the canyon. The ground is covered with red dust, and I spotted the remains of several unmanned space probes that landed or crashed here years ago. I headed straight for the top of the canyon.

Mars is red because the dust and rocks contain iron that has rusted.

DATA UPDATE

Scientists think that there might once have been life on Mars. It may have liquid water below the surface, and it has oxygen, carbon, and other chemicals needed for life. **Bacteria** and other tiny forms of life might once have existed here.

Many space probes, such as the rover Spirit, have explored the surface of Mars and collected valuable information.

Dust storm

I hadn't gone far when a wind started to whip up the dust. Soon I couldn't see a thing. I was scared that I might accidentally step over the edge of the canyon. I stumbled back towards the spacecraft, terrified that I wouldn't find it in the storm. Luckily, I bumped right into our spacecraft. Phew!

Today we landed back on Earth! We orbited a few times and gazed at this beautiful blue planet. Through the white clouds I could see the vast oceans and land. Earth is the best place in the solar system!

Unlike any other place in the solar system, millions of different kinds of plants and animals live on Earth.

Reentry

We slowed the engines and dropped through the atmosphere. Just a few thousand meters above Earth's surface, we opened the parachutes, and the spacecraft drifted down. I stepped out of my spacecraft for the last time. It felt strange that I no longer had to put my spacesuit on.

People need to take care of Earth and stop polluting it so that life can continue to flourish here.

SPACE TIP

Don't think that you can leave a space mission and return straight back to normal life. Your body has to readjust. After being weightless for all that time, my muscles are very weak, even though I used an exercise machine every day. It will take months before they are strong again.

FINAL DATA UPDATE

Earth is the best (and possibly the only) place in our solar system where life can exist, because

- it has plenty of water;
- it has oxygen for living things to breathe;
- it is the right distance from the Sun, so it is not too hot and not too cold.

Glossary

asteroid One of thousands of lumps of rock that orbit the Sun

atmosphere Layer of gases that surrounds most planets and some moons in the solar system

bacteria Microscopic living things that each consist only of a single cell

comet Object in space made of ice and dust with a long tail, which orbits the Sun

crater Hole, in the ground or at the top of a volcano, made by an explosion

equator Imaginary line around the middle of a planet or moon

eruption Sudden explosion outwards from inside something

global warming Increase in the average temperature at the surface of the Earth

gravity Force of attraction between two objects—the bigger the object the stronger the force

Hubble space telescope One of the largest telescopes ever carried on a spacecraft

lava Molten rock that escapes from a volcano during an eruption

meteorite Rock that falls from space on to a planet or moon

moon Large rocky object that orbits a planet

orbit Path taken by an object in space as it moves around a larger object

planet Object in space that orbits the Sun or another star

reinforced Made stronger

solar system The Sun and everything that orbits it, including all the planets, their moons, asteroids, and comets

solar particles Tiny fast-moving, dangerous particles emitted by the Sun

space probe A robotic spacecraft sent on a specific mission to explore something in space

sulphuric acid Very strong acid that consists of sulphur, hydrogen, and oxygen combined

unmanned With no human crew

Further Information

Web Sites

This Web site has been created especially for children by the NASA space agency. It includes games, activities, and lots of information. Follow the links to find out about exploring Mars, the solar system, and much more at:
http://nasascience.nasa.gov/kids/kids-solar-system

Discover information about the planets and their moons at:
www.kidsastronomy.com/solar_system.htm

This is another NASA Web site for children.
Find out about the technical aspects of exploring space at: **http://solarsystem.nasa.gov/kids/index.cfm**

Books

Space Survival Guide by Ruth Owen.
Crabtree Publishing Company (2010).

Space Probes: Exploring Beyond Earth by David Jefferis.
Crabtree Publishing Company (2009).